This is a story about a little orphaned squirrel who came to be known as Theodore. Theodore was about 10 days old when I heard him crying by an old oak tree where he had fallen from his nest.

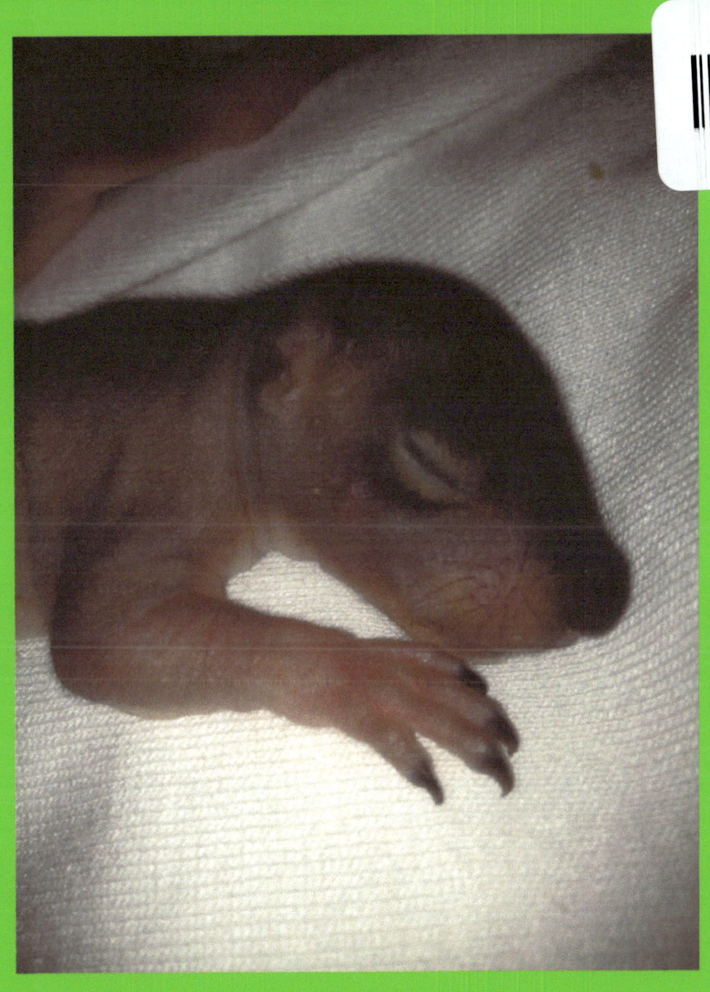

He was cold, hungry and dehydrated. It was too cold to leave him there, so I brought him home to nurse him back to health.

This is Theodore on the day I brought him home.

In the beginning, Theodore was so young that his eyes had not opened yet, and he had very little hair on his body. It was several weeks after I brought him home before he opened his eyes and each day he grew more and more hair.

He was very tiny and had no teeth, so I used an eyedropper to feed him. He loved to eat! However, he was very messy at eating.

He was such a messy eater that he needed a bath everyday. He loved to get a warm bath and towel dried afterwards. Then he would snuggle up under a blanket and fall asleep.

As Theodore got older he started to get his front teeth. I started to feed him mashed up bits of bananas and bread with his replacement milk. He really loved bananas and bread!

Obviously, he was a really messy eater. He slurped and smacked really loud, and he ate really fast. Teaching a squirrel about table manners was not easy to do.

After a few more months, Theodore started to grow more and more.

His tail started to fill out, and he also started eating on his own.

He loved to go outside, play in the grass, climb trees and listen to the sounds of nature.

When he got tired he would climb up to my shoulder and sit for a bit, then he would snuggle up and fall asleep.

Theodore loved people and people loved him.

He would scurry down the tree every time someone stopped to visit, and he would sit on the front porch with us and snack on peanuts.

When he was about 3-4 months old he started eating new foods. He wasn't afraid to try anything new.

He liked fresh fruits and vegetables from the garden. He liked bananas and strawberries, but he didn't care for grapes or watermelon.

He liked zucchini, cucumbers and green beans, but he did not like lettuce or celery.

He tried BBQ chips and corn chips, but he preferred peanuts, sunflower seeds, walnuts, and cashews.

Have you ever wondered, do squirrels eat ice cream? Yes! They do! Theodore loved ice cream and glazed donuts!

He didn't like to eat alone, so sometimes he invited friends.

Sometimes he thought he was human. He would eat peanuts from a coffee cup in the mornings.

He loved to drink fresh water from a glass.

He liked to celebrate holidays.

He dreamed about his future.

He wanted to learn to ride a bike, but the pedals and handle bars were never long enough for him.

I posted pictures of Theodore on Facebook. People loved to watch him grow and see the funny things he did. Theodore liked to look at the pictures I posted.

When Theodore got a little older he built a nest in a tree in my front yard, and he came back to visit me every day.

Now he spends his time playing with his other squirrel friends, and he gathers nuts and acorns and stores them up for the winter.

BEWARE

Squirrels are wild animals.
They are not meant to be raised by humans.
Do not ever attempt to catch or chase them.

Although you may love the story about
Theodore the squirrel,
this was a rare occassion,
and the only way he was able to survive
was with the help from an adult.

Do not ever pick up, touch,
or chase wild animals of any type.

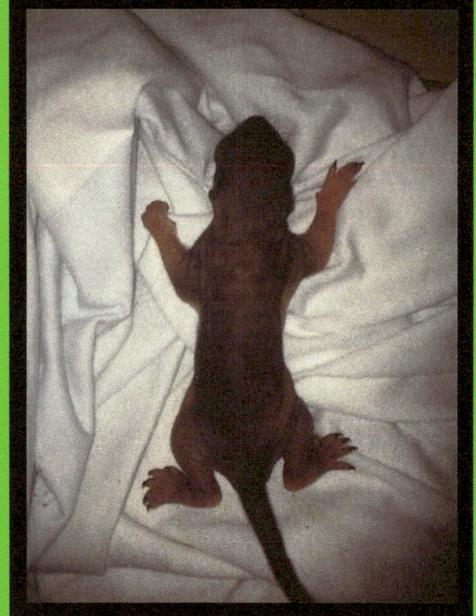

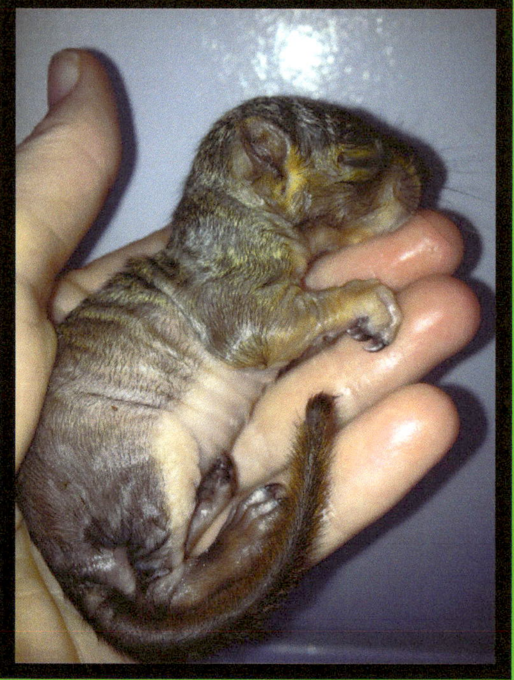

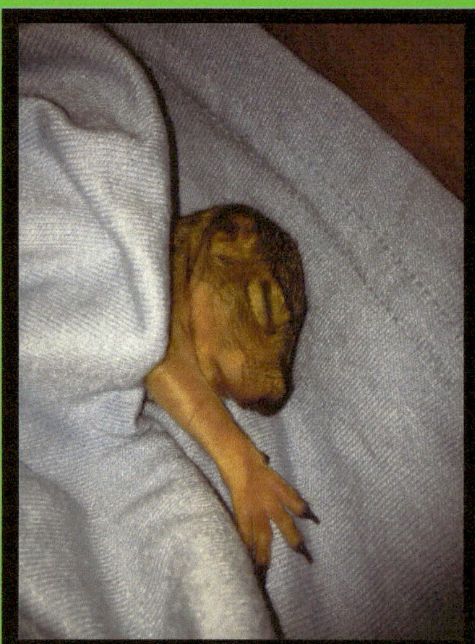

The End

www.ingramcontent.com/pod-product-compliance
Ingram Content Group UK Ltd.
Pitfield, Milton Keynes, MK11 3LW, UK
UKHW060117300726
14090UKWH00002B/234

* 9 7 8 1 4 9 3 6 1 0 5 9 4 *